Coastal Britain

ROBERT HALLMANN
Coastal Britain

TEXT BY ROGER THOMAS

B T Batsford Ltd · London

First published 1984
© Robert Hallmann 1984
Text © B.T. Batsford Ltd, 1984

ISBN 0 7134 3733 2

Printed in Spain by Grijelmo S.A. Bilbao
for the publishers,
B.T. Batsford Ltd,
4 Fitzhardinge Street, London W1H 0AH

Frontispiece: *Brighton, Sussex. The most 'sophisticated and elegant' resort in
Britain, known sometimes as 'London by the Sea', because of its railway links
with the capital, retains its Victorian atmosphere, despite modern development.
The Palace Pier is still open to the public, although the West Pier, much
delapidated, and a challenge for conservationists, has been threatened with
demolition.*

Contents

LIST OF PHOTOGRAPHS

1 The Nature of the Coast

We take certain things for granted. We all accept, for example, that Britain is a maritime country, its history and destiny intertwined with the seas which surround it. We are told, often enough, that Britannia once ruled those seas, in both a military and a commercial capacity. Sir Francis Drake and Admiral Lord Nelson rank amongst the greatest national heroes. At a humbler level, Britain's collective spirit has also been touched by the dutiful Jolly Jack Tar.

It is not an exaggeration to say that the entire national character and culture have been fundamentally influenced, even created, by the sea. The British are, after all, a so-called 'island race', a description that implies, depending on which side of the fence you stand, insularity or uniqueness, xenophobia or pride.

Of all the things we take for granted, the most fundamental is a relationship with the sea. No place in Britain is more than a few hours' drive from the sea. Most of the main conurbations are either on, or only a short distance from, the coast.

An examination of that coast reveals a few surprising statistics. We are constantly reminded that Britain is a small country. After all, the much-quoted distance between John o'Groats and Land's End – a mere 900 miles – is, if you will excuse the metaphor, a drop in the ocean. Yet for such a small country, there is an inordinate amount of coastline – around 7000 miles at the last count.

Massive seismic disruption and the revolution in communications technology permitting, the British will continue

Overleaf: *Land's End, Cornwall. Landfall on a mist-shrouded island. The craggy rocks of Land's End reach out into the stormy waters of the Atlantic; this is the westernmost point of mainland Britain, although on a clear day the Isles of Scilly can be seen, nearly thirty miles away.*

7

Harlech Castle, North Wales.
The sea takes and the sea gives.
Harlech Castle now lies
three-quarters-of-a-mile inland.

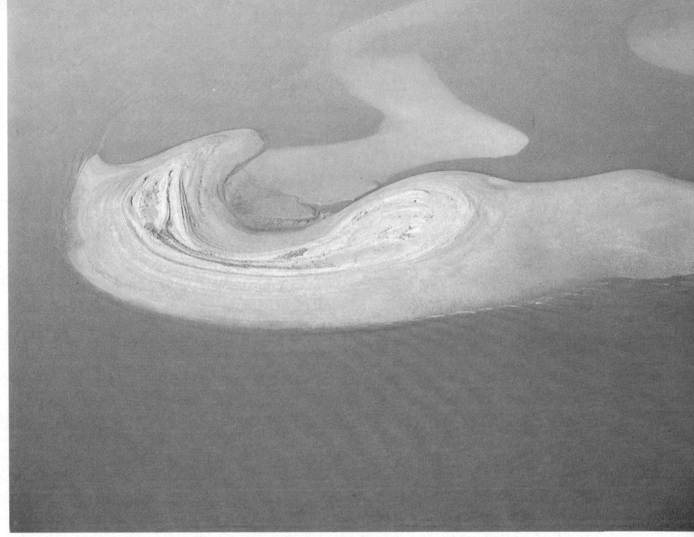

to abide by, and take for granted, a special status as an island people, continue to display a certain atavistic antipathy for deprived, landlocked countries, far removed from the whiff of ozone or the sight of a sea-cliff, still feel sorry for those nations washed only by a meagre stretch of uniform beach and bland duneland. Such feelings are inevitable, for the sea has moulded Britain's evolution as a nation, sometimes protecting, often insulating her from external forces good and evil.

But to begin at the beginning, Britain was not always an island. On the geological clock, calibrated in hundreds of millions of years, the British Isles have been in existence for no more than an instant. Until about 10,000 years ago, Britain was a promontory of north-west Europe. Around that time, the great glaciers and ice sheets covering the land began to recede. In melting, they caused the sea level to rise, and by about 6000 BC the North Sea had been formed, submerging the land-bridge with France. Britain was an island.

The coastline thus created was not something definitive or inviolable. It is wrong to think of Britain's complex coastal pattern in terms of a shape fixed for eternity. Although we humans, with our allotted lifespan of three score and ten, can never hope to comprehend entirely the notion of change as measured by that geological clock, even we can observe changes in the coastline.

Artificial island, Thames Estuary. A man-made island in the North Sea was designed to test the effects of tide and weather near the Maplin Sands, in case London's third airport should ever be placed there.

Opposite: *Warden Point, Isle of Sheppey, Kent. The coastline is ever-changing, the eastern shore gradually losing ground to the sea. Here on Sheppey the constantly sliding clay cliffs demonstrate the effects of coastal erosion.*

Overleaf: *Canvey Point, Thames Estuary. Seen from the air at low tide, the mudflats become a convoluted pattern of rivulets and run-offs.*

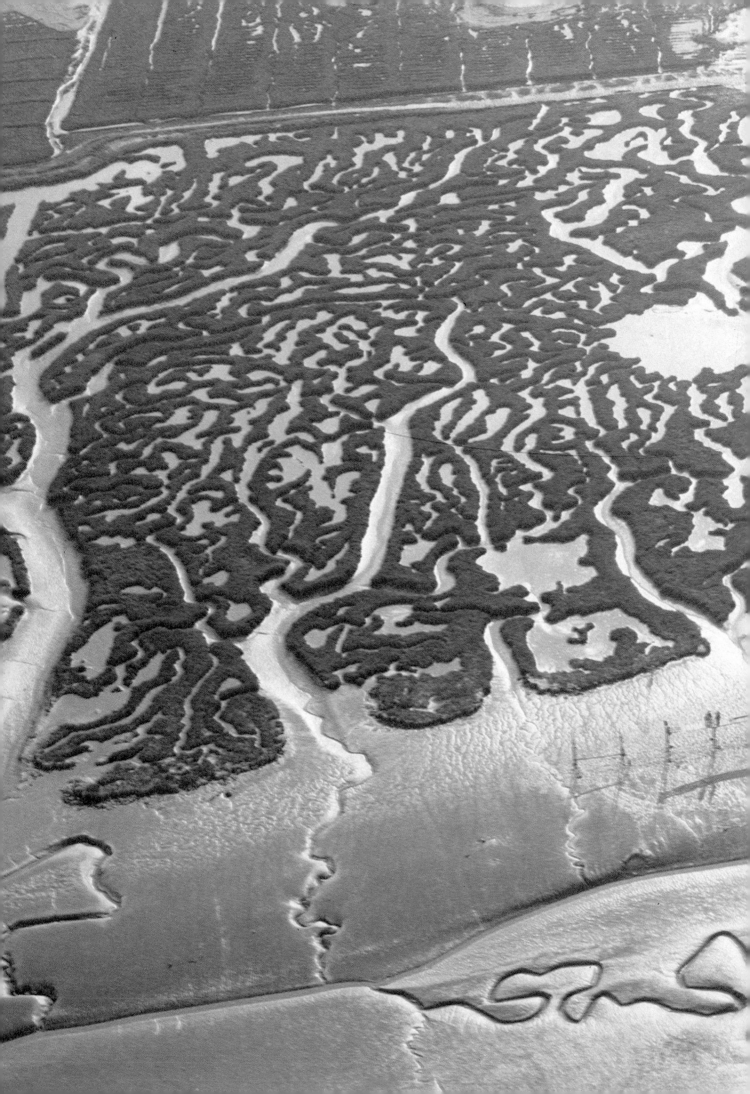

Things happen fast along Britain's seaboard. Land appears and disappears on a human timescale. When the medieval monarch Edward I decided to construct his mighty castle on a rocky outcrop at Harlech, North Wales, in 1283, he made sure – as was his practice – to build it right on the coast for strategic reasons. Soon, the sea began to recede. Now, his 'Way From the Sea' stands beside Harlech's railway station, the distant waves three-quarters-of-a-mile away. A little further south, seabirds still continue to nest at Bird Rock near Tywyn, even though this 600-foot outcrop, an erstwhile sea-cliff once lapped by waves, is now about five miles inland.

On the opposite side of Britain, the converse is taking place. At Holderness in Yorkshire (or, strictly, Humberside) the sea is winning. The victory is so conclusive that here, between Bridlington and Spurn Head, we have the fastest eroding coastline in the world. Every year, as much as six feet of the soft clay cliffs are disappearing, much to the chagrin of farm- and landowners. Clifftop bungalows at Barmston have tumbled into the sea since 1973. A whole string of coastal villages which existed at the time of Domesday Book surveys in 1086 are all now under water. Profound shifts in land-form are not always imperceptible; they can sometimes be measured in years rather than aeons.

Evidence of the constantly changing shape of Britain can also be found at Dunwich. This now-peaceful part of the Suffolk coast was, in medieval times, a thriving seaport and prosperous city. It became a victim of continuous erosion as the sea destroyed its soft, sandy cliffs. By the sixteenth century, its three ancient churches had gone and the sea was attacking the market place. Today, this once-important borough is no more than a hamlet.

Sea became land in the Wantsum Channel, Kent. In Roman times, the area known as Thanet (today with its modern resorts of Margate and Ramsgate) was a true island. The Wantsum Channel, then a sea strait and convenient passageway to the Thames estuary and London, gradually silted up. A covering of vegetation formed over the mud- and salt-flats, and from the twelfth century onwards the 'channel' was finally reclaimed from the sea.

Britain's coastline is full of examples which testify to its impermanence. Seaton and Ravenspur in the north-east of England and the original town of Winchelsea in Sussex are among others that have been given up to the sea. However, it would be wrong to give the impression that the aquatic forces which successfully defied the imperatives of poor King Canute always come out on top. Taken as a whole, Britain's land mass is not being gradually eaten away by a hungry sea. Despite often dramatic erosion, more land is being gained than lost.

The silting process, already mentioned, accounts for much land reclamation; so too does the tilting and raising of the land to create new dry surfaces. Unlike the relatively sudden impact of erosion (another example – the beloved cliffs of Dover are disappearing by as much as fifteen inches a year!), the formation of new land is a

Beachy Head, Kent. A powerful lighthouse, dwarfed by the vertical chalk cliffs which rise abruptly behind it to 534 feet. Beware the unfenced steep of 'Lovers'-Leap'.

16

long-drawn-out process. Over millions of years, the gradual recession of the Ice Age has caused the land, freed from the weight of massive glaciers, to rise. Together with other movements in the Earth's crust, this has resulted in the creation of raised sea beaches, sometimes in 'steps' of two and three (seen to good effect on the Scottish coast). The overall pattern which emerges is that of an unstable coastline. Reassuringly, it is a form of instability unlikely, in any sense, to rock any boats.

In terms of physical features, though, it is quite impossible to find an overall grand design; for Britain has the benefit of one of the world's most varied coastlines. For the coastal traveller, dramatic changes in scenery can occur with surprising abruptness. Beaches will suddenly rise to towering sea-cliffs; imperious headlands give way to tiny coves; duneland becomes swallowed up by salt-marsh; forested mountain-sides look down to sandy estuaries.

This variety, much appreciated – and exploited – by the English, Scottish and Welsh Tourist Boards, is largely due to a corresponding variation in the rock structure exposed to the action of the sea and weather. Britain's geological structure makes it a scenically diverse island almost without parallel. Its landscape contains plains, downs, hills, plateaux and mountains. Its coastline is more variegated still, for Britain's rocks are at their most vulnerable when attacked by the ocean, producing a seaboard which is often spectacular, always inconsistent. In the simplest terms, soft rocks become moulded into bays and inlets between the harder, more resistant rocks, which stand out to become headlands, cliffs and promontories.

Totally different features can be seen on the extremes of England's south coast, the granite outcrops in Cornwall contrasting with the chalk-white cliffs of Dover and Beachy Head. The rocky coast of Cornwall and Devon is under constant attack from the sea. Erosion here can be dramatic, producing a jagged, serrated shoreline. Further east, the action of the sea on the pleasant Dorset coast has been more subtle, though here we can see, in its intriguing coves, perfect examples in miniature of the way in which different rocks react to the pounding of the waves.

Apart from being one of Britain's best-known beauty spots, Lulworth Cove, east of Weymouth, is a text-book example of the effects of differential erosion. Originally, this stretch of coast would probably have been a uniform, unbroken cliff face of resistant limestone rock. Eventually, the sea penetrated the tough limestone. One chink in the armour was enough, for the sea was then able to wear away, relatively easily, the soft clay behind the limestone up as far as a fairly hard band of chalk, thus forming the cove as we now see it.

Another emphatic illustration of the effects of sea sculpture lies a little further west of Lulworth. On the map, the Bill of Portland has a precarious look to it. This pointed little peninsula appears to be connected to the mainland by a thin red line, the A354 bridge

Priest's Cove, Cape Cornwall. Only four miles north of Land's End, the only cape in England and Wales is even more impressive than the 'end of the land', yet it attracts far smaller sightseeing crowds.

Overleaf: Dorset Coastal Path. There are paths along many stretches of Britain's coast, affording marvellous views to the energetic, but never more so than here along the sculptured headlands and coves of Dorset.

19

and causeway. Portland, a limestone 'island', has been isolated due to the complete removal of the soft clays. Man is having more success than the sea in removing substantial chunks of Portland as he continues to quarry its attractive building stone.

The weather, too, plays its part in moulding Britain's shoreline. Cliff surfaces expand and contract according to the rise and fall in temperature, loosening rocks and smaller fragments. Strong winds will also disturb and modify vulnerable surfaces. And rain and sea water infiltrate the cliff structure, widening crevices and washing away material. The Chines, for example, on the Isle of Wight, are cliffs that have been broken up by streams running in steep-sided cuttings in the rock.

This elemental feud between earth and water has fashioned a coastline of infinite beauty. Seven thousand miles is a long way; so for all the modern pressures brought by a growing and highly mobile population with increasing leisure time, and the development of industry and commerce, the coast remains surprisingly intact. Natural beauty is certainly under threat. Any tour of Britain's shoreline will reveal pressure points, victims of the hand of man, as opposed to the forces of nature. Yet the over-riding impression of any such tour, despite the inevitable blots on the landscape, will be a favourable one. Much of the British coast is still untouched, some of it virtually unpopulated and unexplored by the migrant visitors of the new leisure age.

The south-west of England is Britain's most popular holiday area. Red-cliffed Devon and rugged Cornwall, which accommodate millions of holidaymakers each year, are almost synonymous with the sea. Yet they remain, apart from that short, intense period in mid-summer, largely unspoilt, a succession of rocky bays, wooded inlets and sandy coves leading to wild, windswept Land's End pounded by the Atlantic surf. By comparison with, say, the Mediterranean coast, most of Britain's beaches are strikingly clean – and it is the ceaseless, restless movement of tides and waves that we must thank for that.

Near Penzance stands the striking 300-feet-high St Michael's Mount, a *doppelgänger* of Mont-Saint-Michel in Brittany. Once part of the mainland, it is now connected to the coast at low tide by a three-quarter-mile causeway. Penzance is the port for the Scillies, an archipelago of over one hundred granite islands twenty-eight miles south-west of Land's End. The waters around the Scillies are the final resting place for many a hapless sailor. Folklore has it that in past times the islanders would pray for wrecks, an important source of subsidiary income. The best-known harbour in the west, however, is Plymouth Sound, immortalized by the exploits of Sir Francis Drake, and a fine natural shelter for ships.

The richness of natural spectacle along the British shoreline requires of any writer a certain selectivity in highlighting particular areas or features. No one, though, should disagree with the inclusion here of the rocky seascape to the west of Start Point,

Near Lulworth Cove, Dorset. The convolutions and upheavals of the Earth's crust have resulted in some dramatic rock formations, to the delight of today's many visitors.

Devon, a remote stretch of shore piled high with massive irregular piles of boulders; or, for that matter, the precipitously steep-sided coast between Ilfracombe and Lynmouth, one of the south-west's many officially protected 'areas of outstanding natural beauty'.

Outstanding in Wales is the Pembrokeshire Coast National Park, which extends around the south-west peninsula for 180 miles from Amroth to Cardigan. One of the most celebrated of its many splendours is the 'Green Bridge of Wales', a huge arch of rock spanning a foaming sea off a sheer cliff near Castlemartin. This section of coast, adjoining military firing-range notwithstanding, is one of the most awesome in Britain. Nearby are the pinnacles of Stack Rocks and St Govan's Head (with its tiny, thirteenth-century chapel built into the cliff face), all of which can be viewed from the National Park's coastal footpath.

The Green Bridge is a memorable example of the way in which water acts upon limestone rock. The entire Pembrokeshire coast is rich in features which demonstrate its underlying geology. Different rock structures in North and South Pembrokeshire produce fundamentally different coastlines. The dissected, rugged nature of the northern shore derives from intrusive igneous rock. In the south, the influences of carboniferous limestone together with an uplift in the lowland plateau have resulted in towering cliff scenery. And at Milford Haven, a former river valley has submerged to form a deepwater inlet recognized (by, amongst others, Admiral Lord Nelson) as being one of the best natural harbours in the world.

North Wales has a well-patronized, and occasionally undistinguished, coastal strip, though neither epithet applies to the peaceful, cliff-backed Lleyn Peninsula. On the far west of this crooked finger of land, looking out across the dangerous waters of Bardsey Sound to the island of Bardsey, is Porth Neigwl or 'Hell's Mouth', a none-too-fanciful name indicative of Lleyn's rugged, challenging nature. The peninsula is now officially classified – and therefore protected – as an 'area of outstanding natural beauty', a status it shares with the flat, sandy coast surrounding the nearby Isle of Anglesey.

Further north, on the English coast (and perhaps surprisingly close to that most English and most brash of resorts, Blackpool) is Morecambe Bay, a sanctuary for those in search of solitude. The expansive sands here take around four hours to cross on foot, though this low-tide perambulation, from Morecambe north to Grange-over-Sands, should only be taken with the aid of a local guide. The hills of the Lake District are clearly visible from these sometimes treacherous sands. More often associated with lakes and fells, the Cumbrian massif has a windswept and atmospheric seashore. The red sandstone cliffs at St Bees Head, the most prominent cape between the Mersey and Scotland, rise straight out of the water to a height of over 300 feet.

Scotland lies beyond the waters of the Solway Firth. The terrain here is gaunt, empty, elemental – increasingly so the further north

Pendeen Watch, Cornwall. Looking south from Pendeen Lighthouse, derelict engine-houses top the cliffs and red tin ore is awash in the cove.

Overleaf: *St Michael's Mount, Cornwall. The 363-foot granite island has been an attraction since Phoenician traders called here in the late Bronze Age; Benedictine monks established a priory on its summit, and today it is one of Cornwall's foremost tourist attractions. Its tidal causeway was the route for pilgrims from the fifth century onwards. Some of the buildings are relics of the fifteenth-century monastery; some date from the last century.*

25

one travels. The coast surrounding the Galloway Peninsula, for example, can seem positively homely in comparison to the intimidatingly desolate sea-lochs, shoreline and islands north of Oban. Here, in one of Europe's least-populated regions, the mountains of the Scottish Highlands sweep down to the sea. Britain's highest peak, the 4406-feet Ben Nevis, rises close to the waters of Loch Linnhe. Offshore, the wild seas are populated by a string of island outposts – Skye, the Western Isles, Orkney and Shetland. A Roman historian, Caius Cornelius Tacitus, wrote of Shetland almost 2000 years ago: 'Nowhere does the sea hold wider sway; it carries to and fro in its motions a mass of currents, and in its ebb and flow is not held by the coast, but penetrates deep into the land and winds about in the hills, as if in its own domain'.

In describing the Shetlands he captured the spirit of the whole Highland coast. Skye's mysterious Cuillin Hills, formed from tough, igneous rocks, are fringed by a barren, inaccessible shore reached only by boat or on foot. The melancholy loneliness of Wester Ross, best known of all the areas in Scotland for its magnificent vistas and grand settings in a romantic pictorial tradition, acts upon the traveller as a release from the claustrophobia of city life – this is sometimes a barren landscape, sometimes wooded right down to the water's edge, the domain of eagles, shepherds and fishermen. The uncompromising beauty of northern Scotland extends to Cape Wrath in the far north-west. Here, rose-tinted cliffs rise to 900 feet, with views (on the occasional fine days) over The Minch towards the Outer Hebrides. Along many stretches of the coast of Sutherland and Caithness the sea crashes against cliffs carved into black chasms, arches and towering stacks – yet here and there are secluded sandy coves where seals bask and seabirds are rarely disturbed. In certain locations in the Highlands and Islands, low spring tides reveal beautiful pink and purple coral sands – such are to be found on Skye, the Summer Isles and the Kyle of Lochalsh.

Scotland's east coast is tamer than the isle-strewn west, though equally empty and unexplored. From the seastacks of Duncansby close to the surprisingly unimpressive John O'Groats, to the sheer drop of the rock formations at Wick and the bird colonies of the cliffs south of Aberdeen, the coastline is also much more abrupt. The A9, first leg of many a walk from one extremity of Britain to the other, hugs the coastline down to Inverness and offers the motorist many a grand view.

The east coast of England is quite different in its natural character. South of Berwick-upon-Tweed stretch Northumberland's low-lying sand dunes and long beaches – wonderful terrain for the sea-loving holidaymaker, although it can be chillingly windy and exposed – culminating in the sands of Whitley Bay.

Yorkshire, too, offers beaches by the mile, punctuated by literally outstanding features such as Boulby Cliff, where the rock face rises to 666 feet, the highest coastal point in England. Further

Pendine Sands, Pembrokeshire. The six miles of firm, flat, sandy beach saw five successful attempts at the World Land Speed Record in the 1920s – by Sir Malcolm Campbell's 'Bluebird'.

Overleaf: *Loch Duich, Wester Ross. Seen here from Glen Shiel, Loch Duich has all the dreamy grandeur of the West Highland coast.*

south, the stretch between Flamborough Head (with its sea caves and rock pinnacles) and Spurn Head is particularly exciting – the latter, at the mouth of the Humber, ends in a long, narrow and protective sand-and-shingle spit.

The Wash, off the Lincolnshire coast, appears on the map as a square-shaped, blue intrusion into Britain's land mass. In fact – at low tide at least – its 300 square miles of shallows are as much land as water, an area of sandbanks interspersed with narrow channels. Tons of shingle are deposited constantly from the rivers which drain off the fertile Fens, and yet more is carried down the coast from the north by the action of the tide – and so continues the process of reclamation which began when banks were built to exclude the sea from 35,000 acres in the seventeenth century. Two ancient roads terminated at Home-next-the-Sea, now a small, landlocked village: it is thought that the Romans ran a ferry service from Holme to Lincolnshire, at a time when the Fens were still largely under water.

The south-east coast has of course seen intensive development, both industrial and residential, but natural features can still dominate both in fact and in the imagination. Those cliffs at Dover are powerfully symbolic of Britain's identity as an island of which the Continent of Europe has the misfortune not to be a part. Geologically, they are a kind of cross-section of the chalky South Downs as they reach the coast; and on closer examination they are not as spotlessly white as the song would have us believe. From the cliffs of Dover the Continent is not far away – on a clear day you can see it; not surprising, then, that this is one of the main crossing points for Channel traffic.

Although the coastline is more populous around the south-east corner of Britain, it is possible along the Channel shore to find ideal spots for quiet exploration: the Isle of Wight, for example, guards the shipping lane into the Solent, but it is surrounded by pretty bays, creeks, chines and sea caves. To the west of the island, three giant chalk stacks rise out of the sea – they are known as The Needles, probably the most infamous rocks in Britain. The Isle of Wight is, like so many other natural features we have seen, the product of erosion; but in this case erosion not by the sea, but by the river we now know as the Solent, gradually enlarging to a fiercely tidal channel.

Further west is Lyme Bay. Here we should look more closely, examine the minutiae of the British coast. Not only is Lyme Bay a place of great natural beauty; more important, its fragile cliffs and beaches are a treasure chest of fossils. It was no accident that the Darwinian disciple, Charles Smithson, one of the leading characters in John Fowles's novel *The French Lieutenant's Woman*, came to Lyme Regis. In hunting for fossils amongst the blue lias cliffs, topped with sandstone, he could not have chosen a better location, for the Dorset shore around Lyme is noted for its many prehistoric finds. The ammonites here (curled and snail-like in

Druridge Bay, Northumberland. Nearly five miles of beautiful, lonely beach on Northumberland's shore are just part of a rugged and unspoilt eastern coast.

Overleaf: *View from Struie Hill, Easter Fearn. The beauty of Dornoch Firth, looking north towards Bonar Bridge and the distant mountains of Sutherland, seen across the fertile fields and woodlands of Easter Ross.*

33

Sea Palling, Norfolk. Low-lying East Anglia's magnificent beaches are prone to erosion and need to be protected in parts from the assaults of the North Sea.

Opposite: The Needles, Isle of Wight. Probably the most infamous rocks in Britain, the white chalk stacks jut out into the Solent, guarded by a lighthouse.

appearance) can vary in size from half-an-inch to several feet – and are in such abundance that they can simply be picked up off the beach, though the real giant ammonites are to be found in a band of rock strata below the cliff at sea level. The entire length of the Dorset coast is good fossil-hunting country. So too is the Yorkshire coast at Cayton Bay, the White Nab headland and Gristhorpe Bay (all near Scarborough), Robin Hood's Bay and the stretch between Whitby and Staithes.

The clay, chalk and soft sandstone cliffs along the Isle of Wight also yield rich prehistoric pickings. Easily eroded by rain and sea, they constantly expose fresh layers of fossils. Evidence of the doomed dinosaur is thick on the ground; the island claims the largest collection of dinosaur footprints in Europe, with the discovery of around 5000 iguanodon impressions.

Prehistory comes to the surface in more ways than one on the island, for here in a number of places are clearly displayed different layers of rock representing successive geological periods. At Sandown, for example, the rock strata of old red sandstone and grey marls contain fossilized dinosaur bones. This is succeeded by shale rocks of a later period containing fossils of prehistoric sea creatures. The coast between Yarmouth and Alum Bay is one of a number of fossil-rich locations on the Isle of Wight. Alum Bay is, incidentally, also noted for its dazzling variety of colours, a phenomenon caused by the twenty-one different shades of sand in its cliffs, ranging from chocolate-brown to strawberry-pink. (Goodrington Sands, near Paignton, display a similar range of colours; and in the far north of Scotland, at Torridon near Lochinver, the sands alternate between red and jade-green.)

Shells and pebbles are the fine detail of the coastline. Although perhaps a less academic subject of interest than fossils, collecting them is a popular pastime. In variety of shape, size and colour, they are a miniature counterpart to the range and diversity of geological formations and coastal scenery. Pebble beaches, though a little uncomfortable to walk and sit on, are full of interest. No two pebbles are identical, and the pebble collector will have the pleasure of knowing that the smooth, rounded object he holds in his hand will be older than any fossil. The pebble beaches of Norfolk and Suffolk are particularly fine (especially Aldeburgh); so too are the shingle banks between Dartmouth and Start Point in South Devon. The best known of the lot, of course, is Chesil Bank, a pile of pebbles about 16 miles long, behind which has formed a salty lagoon. In the manner of those assiduous flour graders, the tides have washed and sorted the countless millions of pebbles into different and clearly discernible bands of size, small running to large from east to west.

In one final respect, this island coast, with its intertidal mud-flats and salt-marshes and towering cliffs, is another natural – as the habitat for teeming colonies of seabirds. The Pembrokeshire Coast National Park recognizes the fact in adopting the razorbill as its motif; the bird is joined by guillemots,

Camber Sands, Sussex. The desert-like sand dunes are beloved by lovers and film-makers alike; at low tide the water recedes for half-a-mile.

Durdle Door, Dorset. One of the spectacular effects of natural erosion, an arch of limestone rock juts out into the bay from the tip of a headland.

Overleaf, left: *Alum Bay, Isle of Wight. There are more than twenty shades of sandstone – from chocolate-brown to strawberry-pink – in these cliffs.*

Overleaf, right: *Wick, Caithness. The cliff coast of Caithness in the far north-east, home of seals and seabirds, is beautiful in its rugged loneliness.*

puffins, fulmars, kittiwakes and Manx shearwaters on Pembrokeshire's accommodating cliffs and islands.

Further north, where Wales meets England, the sand and silt at the mouth of the Dee is a breeding ground for redshanks, oyster-catchers and black-headed gulls. This estuarine habitat, and that of Pembrokeshire, can be taken as representing the two main categories of shore habitat where birdwatching is at its best, and other such places can be found all round Britain. The coast is of the greatest importance to ornithologists, not just for its length and variety, but because here, at the sea's edge, near-natural conditions can still be found, often remote and undisturbed by the incursions of industry, agriculture, or the tourist trade.

Sea and spray on the north-east coast.

2 Signs of History

Man's links with the coastline reach back beyond recorded history. We can only guess at his motives in first settling within sight and sound of the sea. In later, more familiar ages, he turned his attention to Britain's vulnerable coastal fringes for reasons of defence and attack, building camps, castles and fortifications on an instinctive territorial impulse. It is perhaps too fanciful to attribute man's earliest associations with the coast to some mystical attachment. Base motives and pragmatic arguments may even then have been at work, as they were in later, better documented times. Ultimately, the conundrums surrounding, for example, Paviland Cave on the Gower Peninsula, South Wales, will remain unsolved. One of Britain's earliest prehistoric sites, Paviland is almost in the sea. This inaccessible location, cut off at high tide, was excavated in 1823 and found to contain a skeleton christened the 'Red Lady of Paviland'. The 'lady' subsequently turned out to be a man from the Cro-Magnon (Old Stone Age) period, his bones dyed with a red ochre probably for symbolic reasons.

Prehistoric man seems to have had a predilection for far-flung corners of the British Isles. The wild, remote Orkneys contain some of Britain's richest archaeological evidence. Skara Brae, a particularly prized possession, has been described as containing 'the most striking remains of Neolithic (New Stone Age) settlement in Britain' and is considered unique in northern Europe. Located at Skail Bay on Mainland (Orkney's largest island), Skara Brae is an amazingly well-preserved village, for centuries protected as if in aspic by a covering of sand. It was uncovered not by painstaking scholarship and excavation, but by the dramatic action of the sea over a century ago, when a great Atlantic storm pounded Skail Bay's sand dunes and revealed evidence of sunken, stone-built huts.

More conventional excavation techniques followed, bringing to

46

light an almost intact Stone Age village complex, inhabited between 3100 and 2450 BC, complete down to the original stone furniture and artefacts. Skara Brae tells us much about everyday life in Britain five thousand years ago. Nearby, there stands a monument to man's preternatural aspirations. The Ring of Brodgar, echoing the mysteries of Stonehenge, stands beside the waters of the Loch of Stenness, a 'Circle of the Sun' 340 feet in diameter, with 27 of its original 60 stones still surviving upright from the time it was erected.

Speculative theories concerning our earliest ancestors continue to fill many books and television programmes. When it comes to later times, we are on safer (though often more prosaic, less entertaining) grounds. From the time the Romans arrived in Britain in AD 43 (Julius Caesar had invaded earlier, in 55 BC, but was forced to withdraw), we can begin to attribute the establishment of their coastal camps and fortifications to the straightforward need for security.

In the early days of their conquest, the Romans set up camps along the coast to accommodate their invading armies. These also

Skara Brae, Orkney Mainland (House No. 1). Protected by a covering of sand since the day the settlement was left – seemingly in a hurry – until re-discovered earlier this century, the stone interiors give us an insight into the life of prehistoric man. Carbon-dating places occupation of the site to 3100–2450 BC.

Ring of Brodgar, Orkney Mainland. *We still know so little about the rites and beliefs of our distant ancestors – hence the mystery which surrounds the construction and function of henge monuments. We can but marvel at the organization and effort involved in erecting the original sixty stones – their arrangement mathematically based on the Megalithic yard – and to cut a surrounding ditch into solid bedrock, 9 feet in depth and some 30 feet across.*

Overleaf, left: *Whitby Abbey, North Yorkshire. The gaunt shell of a former Benedictine monastery has dominated this wind-swept promontory above the town and harbour of Whitby since the dissolution of the monasteries under Henry VIII.*

Overleaf, right: *Lindisfarne Priory, Holy Island. Founded in the seventh century by St Aidan under the protection of Bamburgh Castle, sacked by the Danes, re-established as a Norman abbey, and finally dissolved by Henry VIII, the priory gave up many of its stones for the building of a small garrison castle nearby as protection against the Scottish threat from the north.*

served as centres of power from which the Romans extended their influence. Dover, that busy channel port which now acts as a gateway for the modern invasion of Britain by car, coach and rail, contains some of the earliest evidence of the Romans' arrival. They built a *pharos,* or lighthouse, here in AD 43 to guide their ships through the Channel by night. Much of the original Roman brickwork can be seen in the restored ruins, which share a hilltop site above the harbour with the Anglo-Saxon Church of St Mary-in-Castro.

Seaborne access was often taken into consideration by these great strategists. Cardiff's Roman camp, on a site now occupied by the castle, was built on a tidal stretch of the River Taff. This legionary fortress, dating from AD 75, was a substantial, eight-acre affair. Initially a wooden construction, it was later rebuilt as a stone fortress in the manner of the Romans' 'Saxon shore' forts in south and east England.

This evolution from wood to stone coincided with an ironic role-reversal for the Romans. As time went by and they consolidated their authority within Britain, the invaders became the invaded. Towards the end of their rule (they left Britain in AD 383, the Empire in ruins) they were attacked by the Saxon hordes who swept across the water from the lands now known as Germany.

To defend their coastal frontier, the Romans built a string of so-called 'Saxon shore' forts between the Solent and the Wash. At Porchester, for example, they put up a nine-acre fort in the late third century. Protected by twenty-foot walls and a natural defensive position jutting out into the sea, this well-preserved location later became the basis for a Norman stronghold when a keep and walled courtyard were added.

The Saxon shore fort of Anderida occupies a site better known perhaps as Pevensey Castle. More than half of the original Roman masonry still survives, though the Sussex coastline here is much changed: the sea, which once lapped the fort and castle walls, has now receded. Pevensey Castle is interesting as an historical storyboard which tells the tale of almost continuous use and modification over the centuries in response to new, increasingly sophisticated threats. The Romans were followed by the Normans, who were quick to recognize the strategic value of the old fort and constructed a castle here in the eleventh century. In later times, Pevensey was prepared to ward off threats from the Spanish Armada, Napoleon and, in our own century, Hitler.

Other Saxon shore forts which display interesting remains include Reculver and Lympne in Kent (the former partly destroyed through cliff erosion), Bradwell in Essex and Brancaster on the Wash (still under excavation). Richborough, Kent, is also worth a visit. Here, near Sandwich, the Romans established a base – Rutupiae – in AD 43 which served as their chief port of entry during their invasion of Britain. Later, it became a defensive rather than offensive position as the most important of their Saxon shore forts.

St Cwyfan's Church, Anglesey. Built on a rocky outcrop in a quiet secluded bay, the simple little church, with its roots in the seventh century, depended on the ebb and flow of the tide for its times of worship. That was a minor obstacle in the face of the zeal of the early church.

Overleaf: *Bamburgh Castle, Northumberland. The history of Bamburgh Castle is a slice through the history of England. A defensive position even before Roman times, seat of the first Saxon kings in the sixth century, Norman castle, strategic stronghold in 400 years of fighting against the Scots, Bamburgh featured prominently too in the 'Wars of the Roses'. It has been called the best castle in England.*

53

Following the departure of the Romans, Britain subsided into a
'dark age' during which few permanent fortifications were
constructed to protect the coast until the coming of the Normans –
and their stone castles – in the eleventh century. But in this
interval momentous spiritual events were taking place, and these
were responsible in the end for a glorious architectural legacy. The
itinerant nature of the early, peripatetic saints who introduced
Christianity to British shores may largely have dictated a tendency
towards coastal locations. St David (born AD 520) brought the
faith to Wales and gave his name not only to Britain's smallest
cathedral city but also to the rugged Pembrokeshire promontory
of St David's Head. On the tiny Scottish island of Iona offshore
from the Isle of Mull, St Columba founded a monastery in AD 563.
His church, the earliest Christian settlement in north and west
Scotland, later became a Benedictine abbey which was restored to
its former glory in this century.

Dr Johnson, on one of his celebrated eighteenth-century tours,
visited the island. His remark – 'that man is little to be envied
whose piety would not grow warmer among the ruins of Iona' –
will be endorsed by any visitor to these remote, often inhospitable
religious settlements. One consideration influencing their location
was undoubtedly based on the hair-shirt principle – the more
uncomfortable the better. The siting of abbeys on draughty
promontories and cliffs, exposed to the full force of sea winds and
lashing gales, must in some way reflect the zealous belief that
spiritual fulfilment can only be achieved through physical
deprivation. Whitby Abbey, founded by St Hilda in 657, certainly
proves the point. A posting to Whitby Abbey – usually in winter –
was often the method used to punish an unfortunate monk who
had transgressed. The ruined church was 'not so much pulled
down as blown away'. Today, Whitby Abbey, on its dominant
but exposed clifftop retreat, still seems a chilling place – even at
the height of summer.

Further north, off the bleak Northumbrian coast, lies Holy
Island (alias Lindisfarne), linked to the mainland by a low-tide
causeway. Holy Island is thus named as the birthplace of
Christianity in England. In AD 635 St Aidan travelled from Iona to
found a monastery here, later destroyed by marauding Danes. The
Benedictines, who arrived here in the relatively more settled
eleventh century, re-established a religious community by
building a priory, the remains of which can still be visited.

Nearby, two to five miles offshore, is the archipelago of 26 little
island and islets known collectively as the Farnes. St Aidan also
came here in 635. From then on, the Farnes became a place of
pilgrimage and hermitage (their name derives from the Anglo-
Saxon *Farena Ealande*, meaning 'Island of Pilgrims'). St Cuthbert
built a cell here in 676, probably on the site of the present chapel
which dates from the fourteenth century and is dedicated to him.

The spirit which lies behind religious architecture seems shifting
and indefinable. The work of the medieval military architect is less

clouded by speculation and conjecture. His was the hard-nosed world of attack and defence. His intentions were uncompromisingly simple, symbolized by that most powerful of edifices, the stone castle.

The Normans, as every schoolboy is supposed to know, arrived in 1066. They brought with them the technique of building castles in stone. This soon replaced the frail earthwork and timber ('motte and bailey') method, altering the face of Britain forever as permanent, powerful stone fortresses sprang up to defend and protect newly acquired territories. One of the earliest was Dover Castle, begun shortly after the Conquest on the commanding heights above the town, harbour and English Channel.

This formidable fortification (its keep has been described as the strongest in England) has seen service over many centuries, including an unsuccessful attack by the French in 1216. Like Pevensey Castle, Dover has played a long-term coastal defensive role, evolving in tandem with the technology of warfare. In Napoleonic times, for example, it was strengthened with the addition of gun emplacements, and during the Second World War, the castle was again re-fortified.

Dover's history as a port is also an eventful one. It was, in medieval times, one of the Cinque (five) Ports, a powerful confederation of Kent and Sussex ports recognized by Royal Charter in 1278. 'Cinque Ports' is really a misnomer, for there are seven in all – Dover, Sandwich, Hythe, Romney, Hastings, Rye and Winchelsea. Prior to the establishment of the Royal Navy in Tudor times, this confederation provided ships and men to protect the strategic waters of the Channel in return for certain rights and privileges.

Whatever their functional role, or the inevitably bloody deeds associated with their history, castles are now seen as stirring and romantic structures. This is particularly true of Britain's coastal castles, their mature medieval walls standing proud above windswept beach and dune, mountain-backed estuary and placid sea-loch. England, Wales and Scotland all have such castles. They are beguiling places which can subdue the critical faculties of even the most dispassionate historian.

The spirit of medieval romance – as opposed to the always draughty, often dangerous reality of living in the place – is very much alive at Bamburgh Castle, standing on its isolated volcanic crag above the empty sands of north Northumberland. An attack on Bamburgh must have been a daunting prospect. This site, well protected both seawards and landwards, was chosen as a base by the Angles who landed here in the sixth century. Bamburgh soon became the capital of their new Kingdom of Northumbria, though following its rebuilding in Norman times the castle fell into neglect and decay. The castle as it now stands is largely a product of restoration in the eighteenth and nineteenth centuries. Such is the visual impact of its towering red sandstone walls that Bamburgh is now something of a film star, a ready-made set for directors in search of the 'ultimate castle'.

On the north coast of Wales there's something much more authentic, albeit not in such a pristine condition. Conwy Castle, on the Deganwy estuary, is the real thing. Dating from 1282, this castle still retains a medieval air, its eight massive round towers and soaring curtain walls continuing to dominate the attractive little town and quayside that grew up around it.

Conwy is one of Wales's great Edwardian castles, a link in the chain of fortresses built by King Edward I in the late thirteenth century to contain and subjugate the Welsh. Seaborne access was an important factor in Edward's strategic thinking. Any castle thus located could be provisioned by boat in the event of a siege; access by ship overcame the constant threat of isolation in this mountainous, hostile part of North Wales with its difficult communications and overland transport.

Flint, Caernarfon, Harlech and Beaumaris were also built right on the coast; and when Edward could not go to the sea, he brought the sea to him. Rhuddlan Castle, begun in 1277, was connected to the coast by canalizing the River Clwyd for three miles to make it navigable to sea-going ships, a remarkable feat of civil engineering that took almost as long to complete as the castle itself.

In this trinity of romantic castle locations, Scotland's representative must be Eilean Donan Castle. This idyllic location on the west coast, much publicized by the Scottish Tourist Board, combines the ingredients of historic architecture and grand Highland scenery as mountains sweep down to the beautiful Loch Duich. The castle, dating from 1220 but restored in the 1930s, stands on an islet in the sea-loch, connected to the shore by a bridge. This coastal siting, for once, may have proved a disadvantage, for the castle was battered by an English warship in 1719 during its occupation by Spanish Jacobite troops.

Bamburgh's next-door neighbour, Dunstanburgh, is one of those castles whose situation is as impressive as its structure, standing alone on a headland and guarded by a sheer sea-cliff over 100 feet high. Manorbier, on the Pembrokeshire coast near Tenby, has grown up around a delightful Norman castle, built next to the beach between two green headlands. No one who has been here will disagree with the extremely partial description, 'the loveliest spot in all Wales' – credited to its medieval resident and chronicler Giraldus Cambrensis. On the other hand, no one could begin to describe Blackness Castle, on a promontory on the Firth of Forth, in such a flattering vein. This must be one of the most incongruous, unusual castle sites in Britain, for its plain stone walls resemble – by accident or design – the hull of a ship. Indeed, in overall plan, this fifteenth- and sixteenth-century castle is quite close to a ship. Its slightly bizarre profile does, however, belie a serious intent, for Blackness was once a key Scottish fortress guarding an important stretch of water.

The vast majority of Britain's coastal castles were, of course, built for the serious business of defence and attack. Over the

Overleaf: *Dunnottar Castle, Aberdeenshire. This was once the seat of the Kings of Scotland, and the Scottish Crown Jewels are said to have been smuggled out through the English attacking positions in the basket of a fishwife.*

*Castle Stalker, Loch Linnhe.
Now a private residence, the
sixteenth-century castle, built on a
small island in Loch Linnhe, is
the focal point of a beautiful
setting at Portnacroish.*

Martello tower, Folkestone. Martello towers, built in response to the Napoleonic threat of invasion, were luckily never put to the test.

centuries, evolution in weaponry and warfare has inspired corresponding changes in castle construction. In Norman times, fortifications were thrown up to defend the coast and quell any internal strife. Methods of assault in those days were rudimentary, the luckless attacker often equipped with no more than blind faith and a rather optimistic sword or spear.

This all changed in the Tudor era with the arrival of the deadly cannon. In Henry VIII's reign, a new breed of castles sprung up at strategic points along the coast. Built in the 1530s and '40s, they were designed to accommodate a battery of cannons to protect the shore from any attack or invasion by the French. Although we call them castles, these new Tudor fortifications – placed along the vulnerable south coast from Portland to Sandown – bore no resemblance to their medieval predecessors. They were low, compact, circular forts, bristling with cannons mounted on curved bastions.

Walmer Castle, just south of Deal, was one of the major forts in Henry's line of defence. Equipped with three tiers of gun emplacements, it was also one of the robustly-named 'Three Castles which keep the Downs'. Portland Castle, built to guard the harbour in 1540, is still in excellent shape. Designed as a segmented circle with its curved walls looking out to sea, it could accommodate up to 13 guns along its two-storey battery and tower.

Southsea Castle, built in 1544, was the last of Henry's forts. Unlike the others, it has a triangular plan. It is also unique in having seen some semblance of active service, when a French force invaded the Isle of Wight in 1545 (this episode aside, these forts seem to have acted as a successful deterrent in dissuading the French from mounting any full-scale attack on the south coast).

Britain's coastal defences continued to evolve. By the reign of Charles II, any echo of the formal stone castle had been superseded by big gun emplacements made simply from huge earthen banks, lined with brick or stone. Tilbury, for example, was originally one of Henry's forts, later strengthened by Elizabeth I (following the defeat of the Armada in 1588 she issued a proclamation from Tilbury calling on her subjects to resist any further Spanish invasion). In the late seventeenth century, though, this auspicious site was completely submerged by a major new development, an elaborate, tiered system of defences, each bastion providing covering fire for the next.

Britain's island status has probably given rise to a sense of inviolacy which renders the prospect of invasion even more abhorrent than in countries with land-based frontiers. The role of such figures as Sir Francis Drake in the national folklore must be seen in this context. His legendary refusal to leave unfinished that famous game of bowls on Plymouth Hoe before dealing with the Spanish fleet is more a token of a belief in Britain's immunity than of English unflappability in the face of crisis. Apart from a few scares, such blithe confidence has been well-founded. An entirely

abortive and farcical affair, dubbed 'the last invasion of Britain', was conducted by the French near Fishguard, Pembrokeshire, in 1797. The threat of something more substantial and better planned in Napoleonic times prompted the systematic construction of another new line of coastal defences, known as Martello Towers (named after an impregnable fort on Cape Mortella, Corsica).

Positioned along the south and east coasts, they are quite unmistakable in appearance, looking like giant upturned buckets. Over 100 of these squat fortifications were built – often in lines – along the Kent, Sussex and Essex shores during the early nineteenth century. They were, of course, never put to the test; a good thing, for it has been whispered that they are more suited to their current role as museums, houses – even cafés – than to warding off any serious attack.

Occasionally, though, nineteenth-century defences have proved their worth long after their construction. The spectacularly located fort on The Needles, with its complex rabbit warren of tunnels, was initially built in reaction to Louis Napoleon's rise to power in France in the 1850s. It later served as an important fortification giving useful service during the First and Second World Wars. This fort's link with its Tudor or Roman counterparts may seem tenuous, especially when we read, for example, that the first anti-aircraft gun was sited here. The technology of war aside, it shared with them a common purpose.

St Mary-in-Castro, Dover, Kent. The bell-tower incorporates the remains of the Roman lighthouse.

Overleaf: Torquay. *Holiday fun does not stop here with the setting of the sun. Quayside cafes, illuminated promenades, palm trees and a stream of events and entertainments make Torquay the 'Queen of the English Riviera'.*

71

Thames sailing barge. A glimpse into the past – once thousands of these workhorses of the waterways carried their loads of grain or coal on the Thames and up and down the east coast. Now only a handful are left: they regularly 'race' and offer slow-paced holidays.

3 The Coast at Work

It seems strange, in this blasé age of mass travel and international tourism, that as recently as the early nineteenth century an educated adult could, on seeing the sea for the first time, 'not speak till she had shed some tears'. The reaction of this emotional soul, none other than Charlotte Brontë, was typical of an age which displayed a romantic (the unkind would say over-romanticised) attitude to the sea. Apparently, the sea and seashore in all their glory had the power to invoke 'undescribable emotions in the Mind and Sensibility'.

Man's relationship with the coast is not, fortunately, entirely characterized by this falsely sublime attitude. Men live and work beside the sea and have done so for centuries. Most fishermen will agree that there is nothing sublime or mystical about earning a living – a difficult, tough and sometimes dangerous living – from the sea. Docks and ports have grown up as Britain developed first as a great maritime and trading nation and later as the birthplace of modern industry and communications. The spirit of true romance is only evident in the aspirations of the seafaring adventurers and explorers, who set out from the security of south-coast ports on voyages of discovery.

Nevertheless, there was probably a romantic element in the phenomenon which Britain experienced in the nineteenth century: the arrival of the family seaside holiday. It had germinated a little earlier, in the 1750s, when the supposedly therapeutic effects of sea water (to swallow as well as swim in!) were first proclaimed by a persuasive Sussex doctor, Richard Russell. An insignificant little fishing village called Brightelmstone soon reduced its name – to Brighton – and increased its popularity as a spa resort.

In 1783 Brighton received the royal seal of approval when the Prince of Wales (later George IV) paid a visit. Its development since then as a seaside resort has been typical of the many other

Overleaf: Oban, Western Highlands. Set round a large rock-bound harbour, Oban offers rail, road and steamer connections which make it the gateway to the western Highlands and islands.

'bathing stations' that appear regularly along the coast.

Today, although we are told that the traditional family seaside holiday in Britain is in decline, we can still witness the phenomenon of the annual rush to the coast. A lemming-like army of millions still makes the trip (usually concentrated into the few short 'peak season' weeks of late July and early August) and seems to rejoice in the busy, gregarious mêlée of it all.

Holidays are, by definition, an escapist activity. No one seriously suggests that tourists should come to the coast to cast a critical, observant eye on the true nature of their surroundings. To view the coast in a cold, functional light as a working environment is antipathetic to the pursuit of leisure and pleasure (perhaps our escapist holidaymaker also prefers to forget that the leisure industry, to which he is contributing in his role as a high-spender, is now one of the most important sources of revenue and employment for those who live on the coast).

Man has, by fair means or foul, eked out a living on the coast for many hundreds of years. The so-called 'tourist rip-off' of today has many ancient precedents. Smuggling was once a way of life in certain ports, though now it has acquired an almost respectable status as a daredevil, swashbuckling pursuit. Cornwall's reputation as an area of remote coves, creeks and salty old fishing-ports almost rests on it, and places such as Lulworth, in Dorset, where honest tourism is now a staple industry, once witnessed more illicit activities; silent and nocturnal.

As if to legitimize this most clandestine of nautical occupations, Polperro now has its own Museum of Smuggling; though for the first examples of smuggling, we have to return to the times of King Edward I in the thirteenth century when wool was illegally shipped to the Continent from Romney Marsh to avoid the payment of duty.

No self-respecting part of the coastline is without its colourful (and often fanciful) smugglers' tales. Much of the coast also relied on a less contentious source of income – fishing. The great days of fishing in Britain are now, perhaps, over. The decline is a consequence of many reasons: overfishing, the threat from new fishing countries, technological advances, even EEC regulations – all are cited by Britain's beleaguered fishing industry.

Milford Haven, on the Pembrokeshire coast, was once alive with fleets of fishing craft. Nowadays there is only the merest hint of times gone by, when Milford was Britain's fourth most important fishing centre. At one time, its quayside would be piled high with skate, hake and conger. Today, the oil companies have taken over this magnificent deepwater harbour. Massive supertankers now berth next to high-technology petrochemical installations, completely dwarfing the few small fishing craft that survive.

Similarly, places like Fleetwood and Hull – once thriving trawler ports – can no longer look to fishing to provide a significant part of their livelihood. Hull has been particularly hard

Southampton Docks. Britain's major ocean passenger port accommodates every craft from Cunarders like the QE2 to traditional windjammers. All kinds of seagoing cargo and passenger vessels can be watched from its six miles of quays. The passenger terminal here was the European landfall for thousands of transatlantic travellers in the great days of the ocean liners.

Overleaf (pages 80–81): Royal Pavilion, Brighton. One man's dream of a villa by the sea, Brighton's Pavilion was built between 1787 and 1822 for the Prince Regent, later George IV, who made Brighton fashionable. It was John Nash who created this literally fantastic exterior; the building was started in a classical style by Henry Holland.

Overleaf (pages 82–83): Eastbourne, Sussex. Every Victorian resort of any consequence aspired to a pier, and elegant Eastbourne was no exception.

hit by its exclusion from the fishing waters around Iceland, Norway and the White Sea. Like Pembroke Dock on the Milford Haven, its fishing fleet has dwindled to a handful of vessels, though Hull has – again, reflecting Milford Haven's example – been able to diversify by developing, in this case as a commercial container and ferry traffic port for the North Sea. In resorts such as Scarborough, the working ships have long since largely given way to the holidaymaker.

Dorset has one of the few stretches of coastline which still sustains a fairly buoyant fishing industry. Weymouth, for example, that most delightful of south-coast resorts, owes much of its charm to a bustling harbour, full of fishing and lobster boats. Fishing, though, is only one of the many activities which supported life on the coast. If anyone presented a definitive list of the diverse range of enterprises associated with Britain's ports and harbours over the centuries, its reading would tax even the most credulous. A brief resumé would include the shipping of lime, coal and slate, the import of cotton, tobacco and slaves, the construction of timber and metal ships, the building of massive dockyards and the development of mass-transportation facilities for cars, containers, coaches and lorries.

Cardiff's growth as a coal port embodies the spirit of the dynamic Victorian era, when nothing seemed impossible. At the beginning of the nineteenth century, Cardiff was a sleepy hamlet of 1000 people. Within 50 years, it had grown in size to 30,000 on the strength of exporting nearly three-quarters-of-a-million tons of coal annually from its burgeoning docklands. As coal-mining in the neighbouring South Wales valleys continued to flourish, so too did Cardiff. By 1911, the city's population stood at 182,000. Two years later, in 1913, Cardiff docks were acknowledged as the world's premier coal-exporting port, despatching ten-and-a-half million tons of the 'black diamond' annually.

Cardiff's frenetic growth rate was experienced by many other British seaports – Liverpool is a good example – during the Industrial Revolution. Following periods of intensive development, many of these ports consolidated or diversified, so that when the inevitable dockland decline set in, the impetus in the local economy shifted elsewhere. In Cardiff, the old Butetown and 'Tiger Bay' docklands now stand silent, whilst modern office blocks testify to the city's contemporary role as a major administrative and commercial centre. Liverpool's seven miles of dockland, once billed as 'Europe's greatest Atlantic seaport', today play a subordinate role to the city's other industries.

There are interesting parallels between the history of Whitehaven, Cumbria, and that of Cardiff. At one time, Whitehaven was England's third largest port, more important even than Liverpool. It grew up as a coal-exporting port in the seventeenth century, continuing to flourish as an iron and shipbuilding centre in the early industrial era. Although it continues to operate as a port today, the great days of its

84

docklands are well and truly over.

Whitehaven at least continues to survive. Some places never adapted. Their life-spans were short, leaving poignant memories of a briefly flourishing period of prosperity. Porthgain, a tiny harbour on the remote north coast of Pembrokeshire, is such a place. Here, surrounded by magnificent, rocky coastal scenery, there stands an incongruous harbourside ruin looking like a refugee from a nineteenth-century Salford back street. This haunting site is the remains of a stone-crushing plant, for Porthgain was once a quarry port. Nowadays, this unusual little harbour with its one pub and single row of cottages is a popular haven for holiday sailors.

Britain's coastline is dotted with places which have become derelict or deserted by progress on the march. The ruined Botallack tin mines near Cape Cornwall are possibly the most spectacularly located industrial ruins in Britain. In Porthmadog, North Wales, fortune has been kinder. The harbour here was once a busy slate-exporting port. After a period of decline, the tourists began to arrive, attracted by the same narrow-gauge railway – the Ffestiniog – which now carries holidaymakers in place of its

Lulworth Cove, Dorset. An impressive product of coastal erosion, the circular 'cove' is one of the best known landmarks on the South Coast, as exciting for the geologist as for the tourist. Its sheltered beach now attracts the holidaymaker – formerly fishermen and even smugglers found a haven there.

Overleaf: *Scarborough, North Yorkshire. It is said that one used to be able to walk right across the harbour on the decks of ships . . .; Scarborough saw the first 'bathing machines', in the eighteenth century, and it is still a favourite resort of the east coast.*

85

Craster Harbour, Northumberland. The harbour was built originally for the export of stone from nearby quarries; now even the fishing has dwindled.

Overleaf: *Leigh-on-Sea, Essex. Still the cockle boats collect their harvest in the muddy waters of the Thames estuary, but for how much longer? Competition from abroad, rather than water pollution, threatens this traditional trade.*

original slate cargo between the old mining town of Blaenau Ffestiniog and Porthmadog's harbour.

The life of a port is a precarious business, vulnerable as it is to the vagaries of economic change, commercial development – even the physical evolution of the coastline. Many of Britain's great harbours, which played such important historic roles, have relinquished their relationship with the sea. Of the famous Cinque Ports created in medieval times, only Dover continues to fulfil its original role (the ports at Sandwich and Romney, for instance, have been destroyed by changes in the geography of the coast itself).

London's docklands, for centuries at the heart of the country's trading activities, are now being redeveloped as leisure, residential and business areas. Bristol today represents a fine monument to, rather than an active participant in, our maritime heritage. The city, 'still full of maritime history', forged worldwide trading links in wine, tobacco, sugar, even slaves. 'All ship-shape and Bristol fashion' is a cliché harking back to those early times when powerful trading guilds known as the Merchant Adventurers were formed. That pre-eminent Victorian genius, Isambard Kingdom Brunel, launched the first ocean-going screw propelled iron ship, the *SS Great Britain*, from the docks in 1843 (the vessel, salvaged from the Falkland Islands in 1970, is now open to visitors). As at other ports, Bristol's old docks now serve as an attractive recreation area, the working dockland having transferred to Avonmouth.

The hand of evolution is everywhere to be seen along Britain's shores – even in something as unambiguous as a lighthouse. That simple brazier positioned by the Romans at Dover must have been one of the earliest safety beacons. Today's string of lighthouses, positioned at potential trouble spots around the coast, are a little more sophisticated than this Roman prototype.

They are administered – in England, Wales and the Channel Islands – by Trinity House, an organization founded in medieval times. Trinity House was originally a religious guild of Tudor sailors concerned with safety at sea. By Victorian times it had been granted control of nearly all lighthouses, many of which had previously been in private ownership. Today, about 100 lighthouses (not to mention 20 lightships and 700 buoys) are under its care.

The most famous of these must surely be the Eddystone Lighthouse, twelve miles offshore from Plymouth on the dangerous Eddystone reef. The first of the five lighthouses to be put up here was built in 1698. It was a short-lived affair, lasting just one year. Early lighthouse construction was very much a hit-or-miss business; with quite precarious consequences for the poor keepers, for these early models were prone to destruction through storm or fire. Eddystone's 1699 replacement, with ornamental ironwork, balconies and galleries, certainly makes for

Plymouth. Today's private yachts are a small though colourful reminder of the all-conquering sailing ships which once left these waters.

93

interesting comparison with today's robust, functional structures.

The maintenance of safety at sea also depends on the human element. We are all familiar with the deeds of heroism and self-sacrifice performed by the lifeboat service. An early example was set by a woman, Grace Darling, daughter of the lighthouse-keeper on Longstone near Bamburgh. Her famous rescue, with her father in 1838, of nine men from a wrecked paddle steamer off the Northumberland coast is remembered at the Grace Darling Museum, Bamburgh.

Britain, we have reminded ourselves, once ruled the waves. Her navy, although not as all-powerful as it once was, is still the third largest in the world after the USA and USSR, with some 200 ships. Plymouth and Portsmouth continue to serve as naval ports, though there are threats of further rationalization and cut-backs. Plymouth first became the home of the English navy during the Spanish Wars. Later, in 1689, this bond was cemented by the

Harwich, Essex. Ferries and container ships have replaced the once-flourishing fishing industry.

Opposite: *Engine houses, Botallack Mines, Cornwall. A mile down and a mile out to sea – it is said, tin miners could hear the sea moving boulders above them on stormy days. Today the Cornish tin-mining industry is undergoing something of a revival.*

London Docks. The Thames, according to T. S. Eliot, 'sweats oil and tar' – well, it did; today London's docks have lost much of their commercial importance and re-development is likely to bring many changes.

Opposite: *Dungeness, Kent. Two power stations and an old and a new lighthouse share the pebble beach with a scattering of holiday cottages.*

Mumbles, Swansea. The lighthouse on Mumbles Head watches over a beach, particularly favoured with rockpools and all they offer the young explorer of marine life.

Tenby, South Wales. The picturesque old town, partially enclosed by fourteenth-century walls, and with its ruined castle, is one of the smartest and most distinctive resorts on the Pembrokeshire coast.

construction of the Royal Dockland at neighbouring Devonport, earning the area a rather unflattering description as 'the only British city whose existence appears to be centred on war'.

Britain's historic victories at sea are well chronicled and celebrated – nowhere more so than at Portsmouth, which has been a major naval base for over 300 years. Nelson's flagship, *HMS Victory* (built, incidentally, at Chatham in 1768), stands here in dry dock as a permanent reminder of the Battle of Trafalgar of 1805. The raising of the *Mary Rose*, sunk off Portsmouth by the French in 1545, attracted worldwide interest during its famous rescue in 1982. This 'flower of all ships that ever sailed', a great favourite of Henry VIII's, is now being restored for display to the public.

For all its serious commercial and military associations, our view of the sea today is tinged with a degree of frivolity. For this, we may have the good Doctor Russell to thank; though he can hardly have known what he was starting when he espoused the therapeutic qualities of Brightelmstone's sea water. George III

Llandudno, North Wales. Purpose-built for the Victorian holidaymaker, Llandudno, with its elegant seafront terraces, has changed little over the years.

Opposite: *Thorpe Bay, Essex. The quiet end of Southend beach, where beach huts have replaced the Victorian 'bathing machines'. Southend used to be for many Londoners their first encounter with the seaside.*

101

made no small contribution towards creating a fashion for the sea. His favourite was handsome Weymouth where, it is claimed, the first bathing-machine (used to protect the modesty of the swimmer) was baptized in 1763. The trickle of the privileged few soon became the flood of the masses, as the growing nineteenth-century railway network brought town- and city-dwellers to the coast for the first time.

The tradition of the family seaside holiday, although nowadays transplanted to the warmer climes of Spain, Italy and Greece, was born in the Victorian era. Blackpool, the epitome of the gaudy, candy-floss seaside resort, was nothing more than a village in 1840. Now, its 150,000 permanent residents welcome (or tolerate) an annual invasion which, despite recent downturns, is still measured in millions.

The nineteenth-century hamlet of Southend soon received the attentions of the ambitious railway companies – and the newly mobile population of London, who quickly 'discovered' it as the nearest resort to the capital. Llandudno was entirely purpose-built as a resort, its street pattern following the simple 'gridiron' pattern more familiar in New York than North Wales.

Southend, Blackpool and Llandudno share not only a common ancestry. They also have what is for many the apogee of resort architecture in Britain – the pier. In Southend's case, the pier, at one-and-a-half miles, has the distinction of being the longest in the world; though it is distinction enough to have any length of pier nowadays as these grand old monuments increasingly join the ranks of the endangered species. Blackpool, however, still boasts three and Llandudno has one, though its ornate ironwork is eclipsed by the fine examples in Brighton (which has two).

The old, genteel days may have disappeared. Palm Court orchestras and promenading might now be a little *passé* as the bright, brash and colourful move in. At least we have, in the dignified Victorian and Edwardian architecture at many of our resorts, something to remind us of a more decorous time. Llandudno's harmonious, spacious proportions, Brighton's fantastic Pavilion, Weymouth's pretty harbourside and promenade, and Scarborough's spa buildings are tangible links with the *belle époque* beside the sea. In fact, whether your tastes run to the cheerful bustle of Rhyl, or the continental air of Torquay on the Devon 'Riviera', you will find no lack of congenial resorts on Britain's coasts – just so long as the weather holds!

Tourism is not immune to change any more than is the British climate. Statisticians tell us that whilst the traditional British seaside holiday is declining in popularity, activity holidays are on the increase. One index of this new trend is the growth of marina developments along the coast. Brighton's massive new marina, for example, is the biggest in Europe. This man-made yacht harbour, on a 160-acre site which incorporates moorings, promenades, breakwaters and shops, is almost a resort in itself. Although not yet emulated by many other British resorts, it

Opposite: *Rhyl, North Wales. Just along the coast to the east of Llandudno, Rhyl has all the cheerful hustle and bustle traditionally associated with the family holiday.*

Overleaf: *Tilbury, Essex. The industrialized shores of the lower Thames provide a different kind of spectacle as the sun sets behind Britain's biggest container port. The growth of container traffic has led to the decline of the old-established docks up-river.*

102

points a finger to the future. At Swansea, for instance, a derelict dockland site is now being converted into an attractive marina complex.

The appearance of some of Britain's coastline, under the hand of man, is constantly changing. Oil installations and atomic power stations are among the most recent arrivals on the scene. Advances in technology, communications and public tastes threaten an immediate – and sometimes devastating – effect on the coastal heritage. There are – at least in those who administer the National Parks and official 'Areas of Outstanding Natural Beauty' together with powerful organizations such as the National Trust – certain safeguards to preserve and protect Britain's coastline from the more destructive forces in twentieth-century life; and even the forces of nature, as the newly installed Thames flood barrier bears witness.

In the final analysis, man's relationship with the coast must be a benign one. Exploitation and the stimulus of commercial and industrial pressures are inevitable – and will bring inevitable problems. Yet it is possible to remain optimistic. Vast stretches of coastline survive untouched; even where man does intrude, the result may be attractive harboursides, delightful fishing villages and elegant resorts which blend with and, some would say, enhance their surroundings. There is a freshness and variety about today's coast, and we are sure that you will find it reflected in the photographs that have been chosen to make up this book.

Blackpool Sands, south of Dartmouth. A small crescent of white sand, unspoilt and backed by wooded hills, this is a far cry from its brash northern namesake.

Miners' Holiday, South Wales. An exception to the rule? There is a saying that it always rains when the coal pits traditionally close and everyone makes for the sea.

Photographer's Note

I was delighted to accept the commission of producing a record of Britain's shores over the span of a year. I have tried to picture the coast in its differing moods and its many faces and I am pleased that the publishers agreed not to restrict me to the style of the blue-sky picture postcard. Blue skies certainly are welcome, but they're only part of the story.

There are times when the coast is benign and there are times when it takes lives. It is home to many creatures; it has seen the arrival of many peoples, of Christianity and of bloodshed. And it has been an inspiration to artists for centuries.

Time was when only a large-format plate camera would have sufficed for high-quality work, but today's medium-format cameras give us the quality necessary for reproduction, and their portability, together with a variety of lenses and the advantage of roll-films' dozen or so images combine to make them my favourite tool. The ground screen is still large enough for one to anticipate final results. The depth-of-field preview button gives a precise indication of depth of field offered by a given lens at a given setting and the precise effect of lens attachments.

In air-to-ground photography the 90° viewing angle of medium-format cameras seems a definite advantage, enabling you to point and shoot out of a high window without too much discomfort.

My favourite camera – and the one most of my photography is produced with – is the now defunct and much underrated Kowa Super 66, together with 40mm wide-angle lens, 85mm standard lens, 150- and 250mm tele lenses, with interchangeable backs and two bodies. A personal fad? Maybe. But it is usually the equipment you're most familiar with that gives you the best results.

From the air, focusing will hardly be a problem – your subject remaining at infinity – nor does depth of field pose particular problems. It is better to open the lens and increase shutter speed to counter camera shake from engine shudder and wind slipstream.

The lack of TTL metering, on the other hand, is a definite disadvantage in aerial photography, as every angle from a circling plane can give a different reading, particularly over sunlit water. Speedy handling of the light meter and camera adjustment are essential.

Choice of film stock is another aspect of personal preference. The fine-grain properties of a slow film are of obvious advantage. For landscape work I find the cool blues and greens of Agfa 50S transparency film preferable, even though I uprate that film to 100 ASA as a rule. That combination has given me my most consistent results to date, after many experiments and disappointments. Reliability of service and consistency of results are naturally governing factors.

Although a tripod tends to accompany me on all my journeys, its actual use is rare, as most photographic vantage points are out of reach of the car and considerable mileage simply has to be covered on foot.

One advantage of the wide-angle lens is its extensive depth of field, permitting a faster shutter speed, and keeping foreground and background in sharp focus – especially important if it is necessary to pick out some historical or botanical foreground feature. Also there is the possibility of including large areas of sky, should cloud formations or coloration be of particular interest. In confined spaces it may be necessary to use its properties carefully, pointing it slightly downwards to place verticals at the top of the frame and so reduce distortion by converging lines. For a realistic impression it is better to 'waste' the lower part of the frame. Alternatively the full effect of converging lines may of course be used dramatically, as in some architectural photography.

The standard lens is precisely what the term implies – the most common or most used lens: in my case the 85mm. To maximize depth of field I make it a rule to set infinity on the distance ring against the chosen f-stop on the display ring, once shutter speed and f-stop have been determined and set. You can then read off from what distance onwards to infinity your picture will be in focus. For instance at f 22 focus will commence with the 40mm lens at about 1.6 metres; with the 85mm at about 8 metres and with the 150mm tele at about 22 metres.

The longer the lens you use, the more important is the use of the tripod to counteract camera shake. And do not forget to give that extra stop or two to allow for light loss in the longer 'teles'. Experiment will be your best guide for a particular lens, but if in doubt, 'bracket' exposures. Half a stop or a stop either side of what you consider to be correct may lead to just that little improvement when you compare results afterwards – and all you have lost are a few frames of film. As a general rule, when metering the light value of open landscape, choose the middle setting between the highest reading of the sky and the lowest of the ground. Snow scenes tend to influence the light meter noticeably producing an under-exposed result. Take a reading from a neutral grey subject – if nothing is handy, your hand will do – to compensate for the influence of glare.

Saltwater is particularly damaging to the mechanisms of today's cameras. Should yours have the misfortune of a dunking in the sea, immediate rinsing with freshwater and a natural drying process may avert the worst. Prevention is the best solution.

If a scene can be improved with a filter without being intrinsically falsified, that seems to me a photographer's option. The haze-filter may bring just that little more clarity, but more than that, as it does no harm, it stays on most of the time as a protection for the lens.

A polarizing filter reduces glare off reflective surfaces and can add depth and drama to the sky if used at right angles to the sun and it can change the colour of the sea to blue or green. Remember it also cuts light values by up to 2 stops.

Half-grey or half-coloured filters accentuate or reinforce an indifferent sky, but are particularly effective when used *contre-jour* to include the sun. A sepia filter may give a traditional scene a more acceptable overall unity of tone. Artists have always changed a scene to suit their own personal style or their story-telling intent, though for the purposes of this book visual alterations have been kept to a minimum.

Composing the Image
You are capturing a three-dimensional scene on a two-dimensional film. Looking from the air onto tidal mud with its pattern of drainage rivulets, or onto the age-old pattern of man-made fields, stone-walled enclosures or the now rarer hedges, the two-dimensional element is self-evident and the most important consideration becomes harmony – harmony of colour and design. As a rule nature's colours harmonize well – blues and greens, the rust-brown and mellow shades of autumn. But even when they contrast, they tend to be pleasing because they are natural and we are used to them.

Light falling at an oblique angle across a flat landscape improves pattern and texture by lengthening shadows and so increasing contrast, while emphasizing anything raised or indented. So the pattern of a prehistoric site – a collection of low ridges and bumps seen from ground level – can become an architect's layout from above.

Light is the most important and most powerful ingredient in a successful landscape photograph. Use the cool mists of morning to hold together a many-faceted scene or let the late glow of the evening sun suffuse everything with a golden cast. Let the wide-angle lens with a low horizon collect the full visual force of a cloud build-up before a threatening thunderstorm and catch a sparse sun-beam just as it illuminates some important feature in the middle-distance. The trick is to be in the right spot at the right time . . . anticipation!

Patience, too, can be most rewarding. Anticipate the movement of clouds and with patience they can be used to your advantage. Wait for a person or animal to move into just the position you need. Or wait until they have moved and are out of your way . . .

All landscape photography is a matter of selection – selecting the viewpoint, the time of day or year, selecting the ingredients carefully and the light which falls on them – and leaving out anything that is not compatible with your idea for a particular scene. Most unwanted intrusions are, I find, man-made.

Selection can be aided by your choice of lens or the foreground. If an unwanted foreground feature cannot be avoided, deliberate lack of focus may be the answer. The lighter, brighter object is more likely to draw the viewers' attention than a dark one. A bright colour near the edge of the frame will draw attention away from the centre of interest. Strong converging lines – a road for instance – lead the eye through a picture. Ideally they should lead to a point of interest.

Dissect a picture into three parts, horizontally and also vertically. The four points where those imaginary lines cross near the corners are known as the 'thirds'. It is a principle much beloved by camera clubs that points of interest in a picture are most effective when placed at any of those points . . . the 'rule of the third'.

Framing a picture, by shooting through a doorway or from under the boughs of trees for instance, is a good ploy to prevent the eyes wandering off the edge of the photograph and concentrating attention on the main subject.

Should you include people in your landscape? They may be useful to add scale to a difficult environment. But ideally they should be compatible with the scenery – the farmer in his field, the wanderer on the road or the fell, dressed for mountaineering in high regions. Cars can rarely be avoided in urban scenes, but beware : they can date a picture rather quickly.

It has often been said that the best lighting for landscapes is when the sun shines at an angle over your shoulder, illuminating a scene yet affording shadows. But try shooting into the sun and aim for a silhouette – particularly effective at sunset. Bare trees are ideal for such treatment. Nor do you need to stop shooting when the summer colours have gone. Spring, autumn and winter have beautiful, if different, lighting conditions. And there is much less chance of being jostled by your fellow man.